BAD SANDY

CASSANDRA DALLETT

Cover photo by Dante Rouser

Cover design by Rohan DaCosta

© Lucky Bastard Press, 2015

Cassandra Dallett welcomed me to Oakland. She doesn't know that (I guess the secret' out now!) but in that terrifying first week after having driven from Tallahassee, Florida to Oakland, California for my job with Zoetic Press, Cassandra's poems helped me feel like maybe I might just be okay, after all. My first week in the Bay Area coincided with Litquake—a week-long celebration of authors, writing, poetry & publishing that can be a little intense even for seasoned veterans, much less new transplants from the rural south. I remember standing in the front of Dog Eared books with my friend Alex, and seeing a copy of Wet Reckless propped up on one of the tables. The cover art—a heart & dagger with the title, positioned on what appeared to be a woman's clavicle, is what initially drew me to pick up the collection. I remember saying to Alex, as I flipped through the poems, "I don't know what this is, but I need it in my life." Over the next few months I purchased extra copies and sent them to friends from my MFA program, scrawling, "WHY AREN'T WE READING THIS IN CLASS???" on the front pages. The fact that now, not quite a year later, I'm not just publishing *Bad Sandy* with my second press, Lucky Bastard, but writing this foreword, is nothing short of surreal to me.

I can say a lot of things about Cassandra's poetry, and while they'd all be true, they'd all be understatements, too. There's a thrum and a heartbeat to her words that defies categorization. Between the weight and levity of her poetic treatment of sexuality, and the confessional, personal way that her poems are composed, it's no stretch to draw comparisons to her work with that of Elizabeth Bishop, Nicole Blackman, Diane Wakoski, Erica Jong, or Charles Bukowski. Those comparisons—though descriptive—don't tell you the whole story of what Cassandra's work is about. One of the things that as a reader I love most about Cassandra's work is the intimacy of the bond she creates between herself as the poet and you as the reader through the personal mode of communicating. Her poetry is both bitter and sweet in equal measures, so though the worlds she creates for you to inhabit with her for a few stanzas may at times be careening wildly out of control, everything still feels balanced. In *Bad Sandy*, Cassandra examines women as a whole through the specific lens of herself as objects of triplicate significance—denial, despising, and desire—and in doing so, reinvents the world and her place in it. We've all got a little Bad Sandy in us—and these poems teach us that if we put on the skin-tight jeans & leather jacket, it should be for ourselves, not just for the benefit of the Danny Zukos of our lives.

Allie Marini, Oakland, CA 2015

Some years ago, I went to a Grease sing-along at the Castro Theatre, which was about the most fun thing I've ever been to. A lot of people dressed up as characters from the movie, my girlfriends and I noticed that no- body dressed as Good Sandy, but everybody wanted to be Bad Sandy. I said to my friends, "Maybe we should start a band called Bad Sandy," but I don't know how to play an instrument, and can't hold a tune, so that didn't happen.

Recently, the guy I'm dating told me his first crush was Olivia Newton-John. I was all grossed out thinking about her song *Let's Get Physical*, but then I asked him if he meant Good Sandy or Bad Sandy and he was like, "Bad Sandy of course!" I thought about how our whole generation grew up wanting to be Bad Sandy.

Since I needed a place to put my love and sex poems, which I was told were too "Dear Diary", I figured they should live in my Bad Sandy fantasies, so here they are. Until I started writing, I never wanted to be anything but a bad-ass Sandy with a bad Danny of her own.

The poems in this collection are not in any particular order. They were written over the past eight years, so they aren't telling the story of one relationship and break-up, but of many. These poems tell the story of a woman who comes to find that it wasn't really a Danny Zuko she needed to love her, but her own sweet-crazy Bad Sandy self.

Cassandra Dallett
Oakland, CA
2015

The book is dedicated to Lucky Bastard Press for believing in me and the whole Beast Generation, a family of writers that includes SB Stokes, Mk Chavez, Joel Landmine, Zarina Zabisky, John Panzer, Simon Roghe, Tomas Muniz, Joe Clifford, William Taylor Jr., Paul Corman-Roberts, Missy Church, Holly Hardy, Fernando Miesenhalter and a shitload more amazing writers who have been supportive, inspiring and who will probably bitch at me for not mentioning them here.

INDEX

1. 5150
2. Made This Way
3. Periodic Fits
4. The Summer Before I Started Public School
5. Sorrow Is My Only Weight Loss Plan
6. Baby I Was Born To Run
7. A Song Is Playing
8. Predator In The Fish Bowl
9. As We Lay
10. Back Bone
11. Dear Locksmith
12. Aspirations
13. Gaggermeister
14. He Just Don't Understand
15. Kitchen Guy's Magic
16. Hold Back Stop
17. I Cut You
18. How To Out Drink A Drunk
19. Hunter Gatherer
20. I Know I'm Addicted
21. That Girl
22. If You Can't Stand The Heat
23. In The Pit
24. Incandense
25. Love And Other Blood Sports
26. I Been Lonely
27. Making Love To The Minotaur
28. I Am The Lobster
29. Found A Pawn Slip
30. Moist Petals
31. You Purple
32. Of Bushes And Wood

33. Whale Fall
34. Wet
35. Waking On Empty
36. Under The Covers
37. Un Friend Me
38. The Make Out Room
39. The Lonely Hunter
40. The Dress
41. Speaking To You Is Like A Fox News Interview
42. Six Is The Nine
43. Scars Are Sexy Ask Anybody
44. Ripping Up Marriage Material
45. Queen Frostine
46. Problematic
47. Organ Donor
48. Ojos De Leon
49. Frosting The Cold
50. My Ears Are Up
51. My Baby Daddy
52. Begird
53. Black Hole
54. Can't Hardly Wait
55. Curled To The Floor
56. Fallen Fruit
57. Ferine
58. Fly Up
59. I Have Known Lonely
60. I Know I'm Addicted
61. Kill And Save
62. Labor Day
63. Lay Down With Dogs
64. Locked And Loaded
65. Losing Feathers
66. Mount Diablo Is Burning
67. Muscle Shell
68. The True

69. My Neck My Back
70. My Numbers
71. Pushing Plastic
72. Teeth
73. Take Me To The River
74. The Spook Inside
75. The War I've Been Waging
76. Today It Rained hard
77. Vano's Release
78. No Wedding Just a Funeral
79. When I Was Thirteen
80. He's Right I Do Hate To Talk About Money
81. There Are Words People Like In Poetry
82. How Poetry Ruined My Life
83. Falling Into Light Head
84. On Things I Did Or Did Not Do
85. Some Kind Of Way
86. Space Creates Desire
87. Star Destroyer
88. The Skeletons In My Closet
89. The Scene 1985
90. Revolutions
91. With The Walls Knocked Down
92. Pop Corn

**Grateful acknowledgements
to the editors of the magazines, where these
poems first appeared in some form or another.**

"5150," *The Circle Review*
"Some Kind of Way," *The Bicycle Review*
"Revolutions," "Ripping Up Marriage Material"
Rusty Truck
"I Know I'm Addicted", "How To Out Drink A Drunk",
"Sexting", "Confestimony", "Combustion"
Horror Sleaze Trash
"Scars Are Sexy Ask Anybody," *Luciferous*
"Queen Frostine", "Predator In The Fishbowl", "Dear Locksmith", "Hold Back Stop", "Love And Other Blood Sports", "The Dress" *PoeticPin Up*
"Frosting The Cold" *1/25 Magazine*
"My Baby Daddy" *Nibble*
"Ferine", "The Dress" *The Meth Lab*
"Moist Petals" *Black Listed Magazine*
"You Purple", "Pop Corn", "Six Is The Nine",
"Speaking to You Is like Fox News" *Lustre*
"Of Bushes And Wood"
Sparkle And Blink & Red Light Lit
"Waking On Empty", "Under The Covers", "Wet"
Red Light Lit
"If You Can't Stand the Heat"
Red Light Lit & Five Quarterly
"Making Love To the Minotaur"
Sparkle And Blink
"Un-Friend Me", "As We Lay" *Samizdat*
"The Lonely Hunter" *Tres Corezones*
"A Song Is Playing" *TheLegendary*
"Dear Locksmith" *Eleven Eleven*
"Back Bone" *Deuce Coup*

"Periodic Fits" *Kleft Jaw*
"He Just Don't Understand" *Poetry Super Highway*
"Kitchen Guy's Magic Wand", "Losing Feathers", "Of Bushes And Wood", "Take Me To The River"
Pink Litter
"Losing Feathers"-Poised For Flight Anthology
"That Girl", "Practical Nursing", "Aspiration"
Gutter Eloquence
"In The Pit" *The Criminal Class Review*
"Incandense" *Black Heart Magazine*
"Whale Fall" *Van Gogh's Ear*
"Queen Frostine" *13 Myna Birds*
"Ojos De Leon" *Back Room Live, & Yellow Mama*
"Found A Pawn Slip", "The Spook Inside"
Napalm And Novocain
"Begird", "Problematic", "Queen Frostine"
Rolling Thunder
"Queen Frostine," "The Makeout Room," "Hunter Gatherer", "Waking On Empty," "Wet"
Bad Girl Tales Anthology
"I Cut You" *Drunken Absurdity*
"Organ Donor" *The Delinquent*
"He's Right I Do Hate To Talk About Money"
Be About It

5150

Juvenile Hall's walls
are scribbled with the tags
of thousands of minors
in the dark underground
like coal miners in this system
of pain compression depression.
Life being so freaking hard
that turning into an adult
is enough to flatten, to fatten, to addict,
just takes a prick
and see if you can make it through
the transformation.
Not that you'll come out a butterfly,
more like a housefly
that wakes up one day and say,
Shit, I'm thirty
'cause that's all growing up really is,
survival.
The ache of muscles rip-stretching off bone
yearning to feel all this bullshit love
we hear about in songs.
To hold on to whatever it is
that makes us not be a sellout
to grown up attitudes.
To hold on to the anger that runs deep
drives us awake and asleep.
Leaves scabs and sores, pus
 just mother-love pulled off
raw and bloody like all our interactions
at times when just sitting in class
just missing the line of fire,
fists, guns, and that first big inhale on the blunt
the mushroom cloud of dope, is too much.
This mother ain't saying you'll be a dope fiend

cause you tried pot,
I'm just saying that if you make it through
without alcohol, cocaine, heroin, pills,
ruling your rotting premature body
you'll be doing better
than most of the people I know.
But drugs are not the only obstacles
on this course just some of the mud
that sticks to your knees
as you wiggle-worm through the muck.
Stomp combat boots into tires
that threaten to trip and strangle you
with loving the wrong, oh so wrong
teen-drama-queen.
pounding abusive first loves and rides to jail
'cause you can't, you just can't leave her alone
and stop climbing through her window.
Keep your dick in your pants
avoid heartbreak, gonorrhea,
and babies having babies
that feel as grown as King Kong on a building
snatching planes from the sky
inside we're all just little 'ole monkeys
rattling the cage.

Made Like This

When I was little,
I spent afternoons on my parent's bed
looking through Playboy and Hustler,
before I could read, I studied the
pictures, clicked my tongue wetly.

Our neighbor's family had six boys
I rode to school
in their green station wagon
went home to straddle and hump my pillow
smother my face breathless
imagining us in the woods
on a frayed plaid cot
above the mossy rocks
them taking turns with my body
doing all the things I saw in the
magazines,
all the hollering I heard in the night.

Periodic Fits

Last night I texted four men:
two of them ex's,
one of them married.
One of the four informed me
we share a moon-in-Gemini,

whatevs, I said...

This would explain many things, he said...

I was only texting to ask about his favorite sex club.

I looked it up; Google says we share a rapid speed of
thought, vanity, a desire to make many things all at once.

Our emotions are very changeable, it says.

I say the only sin is doing a thing that you know is wrong.

Sexting with married men may or may not be
a thing that is wrong.

Restless is what it says about us.

I believe in Happy Endings, not in fairy tales or relation-
ships but in massage parlors.

Doesn't monogamy sounds like monotony?

We struggle to maintain our independence.
Our feelings are held in too much scrutiny.
A direct need to speak the truth.

   Tonight on stage

I will spill secrets down my shirt,
purple like wine
I will kiss and tell.
I will call it poetry.

Springs are scarred into my fallopian tubes.
tiny fruitless trees prevent the eggs
falling failing little Pac Man.

I almost married one of the four.
He was a teacher.
He taught me to run.
He was the moon-in-Gemini Cancer.
Cancer is what it felt like most.

A cancer that picked my bones
left me starving,
a beautiful carcass I was.

They never stop, it says
reading, thinking, talking,
they never stop….

They often come off as fickle,
that's what it says about us
I text the teacher.

The Summer Before Public School

These girl were at our house
I think they were cousins
with hippie parents like mine.
We were having so much fun
being real girly girls
I was wearing a half top
with little cap sleeves and my belly out.
We hiked up the rocks
at the end of the trail behind the spring
At the top we were suddenly covered in stings
like hitting an electric fence, our bodies tingling and goose-
bumped
We couldn't really see through the cloud
and were just running as fast as bare feet could down rocks
screaming and thrashing
All I remember is a blur of flying black
the woods whizzing by
and the soft bodies of bees in my hands
as I crushed and threw them off me
the chill of each stinger an arrow to my core.

We burst out of the woods
my mother met us at the front door
stripped us of clothes
and tossed us three girls
naked in a tub of baking soda
arms and legs pocked with black venom sacs.
That's how I started a new school,
marked and itching
six inches taller and fifty pounds heavier
than the other kids.
I was a freak who couldn't read

but relished the sound
and knew the meaning of the word fuck.

Sorrow Is My Only Weight Loss Plan

I'm swinging a hammer at his windshield,
he's trying to run me over
I'm in my underwear in a blizzard
his car hits the light pole
tires spin out in the snow
I'm screaming at him to remember this,
remember me
next time you cheat on your wife
not sure if I'm a victim or a victor
so sure I'm nothing
as quick to melt as flakes on bare skin

It's the last I see of him
a man I thought I loved
The lovely starving I did after
the liquid diet tears and beer
a grinding ball
of hated flesh and lonely bones
no part of me could see
past him
with his skinny wife
on the phone
telling me she's his wife
she'll forgive him
they have a child
I held her daughter once
pretending I'd give her a sibling
I will ever smell
the milk spill in his backseat from when she wrecked it,
the day he wasn't at the Hospital door to pick me up,
the crushing cold snow banks outside the heated automatic door

no phone in my apartment
how I lost everything
and dreamt of redemption through love
love for someone too drunk to own it, or return it
who would forget me quickly
settle back in his dysfunction junction

I had no business losing my cute quiet boyfriend for this
turning him into a domestic violence case
at nineteen
making him homeless cause he couldn't love me
 or just say that he did

I wanted proof
in all my black-eyed head-banging
all my hammer slinging knife wield
I was looking for proof
maybe that I was real not so fake and empty,
not another snowflake melting in spring
I was twenty-five but
not sure I'd been birthed
unformed and fetal
trying to swim upstream
God its ugly out here looking for love
and so, so cold.

Baby I Was Born To Run

As soon as I learned to walk,
stripped my clothes off
into the woods I'd go
my nakedness on the mossy rocks
and the needle pine beds
My parents were high, a kitchen full of fools
with six packs and joints to smoke,
and I would be out there
in the leaves the dappled light
I knew the names of Jack-In-The-Pulpits
and Columbine
the places where trees grew close around me
played in empty hunting camps
and abandoned cars
my runaway episodes were legend
a crowd of long hairs fanning out
calling my name down the road
and through the trees
they'd find me curled like a fiddlehead
sleeping under the ferns by the pond.

A Song is Playing

The singer claims
he is a good disease
and this is not the first time today
I think I should start writing songs.

This patch of sun on my back
is pure sex
and reminds me
all that I hate is cold
snow,
shade,
Ikea furniture
and its wordless instruction.

Predator In The Fish Bowl

It's easier when they hit you,
I told the broken girl at the meeting last night
at least you know what to do.
You call the cops even if you still love them.
You know you have to leave.

But when they use words as fists
to pound you into floor boards
crack sharp cheek bones with sneaker treadsoles
text you throughout the day
with knives of judgment
there is nowhere to hide.
You question yourself,
wonder if the things they say about you are true
You feel small, everything you've told them
every detail of self in confidence,
they use as a toothed saw,
dissect you with misdiagnosis
call you the manipulator
when they are losing control.

I know about this torture technique –
texts from ex's, I hug her and say
call me, text me, anytime you feel like it
her body and face gorgeous,
dark framed eyes and square jaw
a perfect pit of beauty
men have smashed and possessed.
She stands there shaking
no less in withdrawals than any junkie
but she's here, in a room of women
hurt but fighting
and she doesn't want to leave,
sit in her car, scared to look at the phone screen

scared to put key in ignition
drive home to an empty house.

I'm scared to go home too,
where he thinks I'm the abuser
who will plunge him back to streets and needles
to hotel rooms in the Tenderloin.
Where he will villainize me
because I can't fake happiness
or orgasm.

As We Lay

And lay and lay
somewhere someone
is getting a slow screw
not here
here you snore
and I rearrange pillows
think about rubbing one out
somewhere they are listening to water
instead of bad television
somewhere they will wake up
wet mouth
on hard body part.

Here everything is hard
and not in a good way
hard like backache
old mattresses
lost jobs and missionary position
is it called missionary position
cause missionaries did it,
or cause it's a fall back?

I'd like to fall back on it
but not till after
I cum.

Back Bone

when you offer
to massage out my aches
I picture you
unzipping my greasy body
you rub each organ
squeeze their toxins
into a trash can pulled close
your strong hands
take up the still small uterus
milk out the embryo
like a pus-filled pimple
you reach deeper
past viscous reds and purples
remove each disc
file and paste
rotten cartilage
gently blow off bone dust
and put my pieces
together again.

Dear Locksmith,
You Look Like Ice Cream

Hear me
bathe you with my tongue

sneak past the cochlea
hammer your drum

tips of my fingers
find your fur

dig the un-inked freshness of your skin
the spotty red of your chest
like mine

I seek out the place where hair meets neck
crisp cut

 I dive in
again and again

hungry for the thickness
the soft crush

you smell good
eyes with so much
gold infused

make me want to become one of your keys
the one that opens your dead bolt

slips in rushing through aorta and ventricle
blue rivers turn red

but I'm just waiting for your face to open
just want to lick your smile

melt the sweet I'll milk from it.

Aspirations

Cold Jelly on vaginal lips
turn of the screw
metal bills push against meat
gauze on cervix
a place never meant for something so dry
pin prick and the taste of numb
Vicodan-Adavan-Motrin cocktail
It helps to forget little bean
the smear of him
we were all this easy to snuff out once.

These days, they use a large syringe
abortions have come a long way
the horror of the vacuum sound is gone
the carved out feeling of a Halloween pumpkin
it's a hard squeeze of the nurses hand
pain pain pain cramping
the Dr. counts it down
gives a light pat, a kind word and it's over
a small bit of blood underneath
you sit up and dress
get your crackers and ginger ale
your day after pill
and out the door
on your way
to do it again.

Gaggermeister (for Sam Benjamin)

I'm still wrestling with this man's story
his agonizing, his love for a porno
a porno that it's hard to believe is even legal
it's apparently legal because it's a series
and in this series, different girls
are on their knees, mouth on dick
in close ups,
the girls don't suck the dick
they are force-fed the dick
throat-fucked, gagged, sometimes they puke.
Sometimes the guy with the dick slaps her face
It's called Slap Happy.
Sometimes he writes on her face
with magic marker
things like slut, bitch, cocksucker, whore
when he cums, he doesn't do it sexily
he does it violently.

All kinds of lines have been crossed here
all sorts of things that any man watching knows
make it a snuff film
snuff cause the girl may be living
may have pocketed a few grand
and went on her way
but maybe a piece of her dies.
every time some loser
jacks off to her gagging, markered face
with each slap, a scar is raised
out of sight, down by her large intestine
snuggled up to her pancreas.
Maybe it will bitter into hate
manifest as cancer
who knows the real damage.

But I'm not mad at this guy

a little horrified that he is turned on
that he jacks off to this mess on screen.
I'm not mad at him 'cause he's honest.
He admits girls like this,
 little blonde things with skinny legs
snubbed him in high school
that he wanted to see them gag on his dick.
(Which, I'm sure he imagines is as big as the guy's in the skin flick)
I feel sorry for him.

He admits his obsession and loses his good girl.
Who was perfectly happy
to give an honest blow job
but get slapped in the face dude, really!?

Still, I want to drop him a line
wonder if we can get down to the bottom
of why we are all so fucked up.
Why I hate fucking my boyfriend
because he isn't aggressive enough
yet he watches rape porn on my computer
when I'm not at home.
And how I hate sucking his dick
its too big and he's too unresponsive
Yet I love the whole face fucking
forced gagging thing
as much as the next guy.
I've watched Slap Happy myself on occasion.

I was watching a scene in a regular movie the other night
where the guy had a belt around the chicks neck
and it was hot and I was totally turned on.
Maybe we could talk about what it wouldtake
to make the perfect porno or the perfect love
where our quirks and obsession blend

into something sweet.
Something that doesn't leave us
heaving up guilt
or broken as yesterday's turkey carcass.

He Just Don't Understand

when I run to the kitchen
throw things
smash chairs
dishes
the wooden rungs crack
I splatter hot sauce
on the cabinets
long to throw it
in his face
and I chant
you have no idea
you have no idea
no idea how crazy I am
while I break up
my own shit.

Kitchen Guy's Magic Wand

He cast it on me
with his stick
or kiss
or odd, skinny frame
something is wrong with his arms
the top part is too short
the shoulders don't turn right
and he walks around like a scarecrow
his face is scarred from shaving
and now
a missing front tooth
still I want to drink him
melt at the feet of his bony little body
nappy pubes he shaves off

I would stuff all of him inside me
walk around like that
pussy, full of him
fat thighs pushing him deeper
pressing my cervix
filling me
the way he does
things are heightened when he's inside of me
words come out of my mouth
that I don't recognize
hungry, horny words
this stream of breathy words
is part of his spell.

Hold Back Stop

Soon as I mailed it,
stuck my hand in the blue box
a greeting card stuffed with scribbled pages
the angsty feeling rose up
questioned, what it is I want from you?
what makes me think I can get it?

You are not a man of letters
of telling your feelings
those doors need to be re-keyed
damned the door jamb
tucked the icky bits
into the inner sleeve
and like most guys
you probably didn't tell her
till hers was closed to you as well.

Twisted ear of key or shoulder
no entry no she said no, no, no, no
she didn't want to talk to you ever
you took a scalpel to yourself after that
cut away pounds of flesh
inside yourself sawing.

Every day at work
fixing lock and latch
sliding metal against metal
with graphite lubricity
drill pin, cylinder slide, hasp and staple
How can a man be so handsome
while eating his own guts?

Working to be impenetrable.
building up your body krypton hard.
Locking dogs at the heel and toe of the shackle
horizontal, to prevent the barking of knuckles.
Oh, the tumblers and shoulder shank,
striking plates,
the keeper and the keep, the differ,
and the follower hole.
A one sided action,
a one sided lock, a plug pin release,
a night latch, safe and vault.

And here I come with a lock pick
and a tension wrench
spring steel hacksaw blades and piano wire.
Searching for unauthorized access
writing these stupid not really love letters
I hang my head
swallow crack-voiced and try
I don't know what I'm asking
I just want in.

I Cut You

with small slices
though my blade was dull
I was relentless
as the slices tried to heal
I massaged them
alternately
with salt and kisses
you found ways
to bandage yourself
salve in other women's admiration.

Your skin glowing red gold
That morning, I found you
in the guest room
looking fresh out' the box
the type of guy I would seduce
not the puffy face at my bedside bearing coffee.
Your white undershirt
clung to you like a teenager's
tiny waist and bulging chest
invitingly rolled into itself.
Face innocent, childlike
the one you slept in when I was falling for you
before we learned to roll to our separate edges
backs to each other.
In those boyish grey shorts
and matching converse kicked off at your side
you were absolutely desirable
legs thrown out
like our big dog does.

You were not mine.

I could see you through her eyes
that's why I picked up your phone
with all certainty
scrolled the numbers
all women
I knew this day would come
that I would have to share
you now that rarest of things
a black man
hetero mostly monogamous
a sober un-incarcerated father in his thirties
with a job!

I have patched up
the many places you were leaking
Then pushed you off
more like a tire swing
than street ready
swinging back and back
hitting my stubborn shins
and insisting that we could survive this
But I kept up the pushing
till you were attached
to a brand new car
you rolled off the show room floor
I sit flattened and cry.

How To Outdrink A Drunk

It's no fun with you.
I can't outdrink you, I've tried.
I monitor the redness of your eye,
the way your cheek squeezes up your face.
Watch for the tone to change
your words to ring with distrust,
subtle at first.
I become a loose woman
more whorish
when actually my body and mind become frigid
now untouchable
One too many and this will be us
deranged.
These nights, I carry a bat
scream, *I Hate You*
spit speckling your red face.
Push you out the gate
lock it.
You climb back over
the fence points leave bloody gashes
in your golden skin.
You plead at my bedroom window.
I wrap myself in blankets
go to another room,
I still hear you.
You are sorry now
you ape baboon.
If I do drink with you
I get mean as well.
I won't just tell you
I hate you
I'll yell the reasons

(I'm a list maker by nature)
kick you in the gut
you lose balance, fall over a chair.
You are huge, muscular
but I'm fueled, venomous
and when I'm angry,
I don't scare.

Hunter Gatherer

The imprint of you on me
looks like hunger
I picture your tiny body
a swirl of hair climbing up your frame
how you look splayed across your king-sized bed
like that pheasant at the fancy place we ate your
calves and biceps small in my hands
so wanting of my teeth
your stomach and hips
swallowed up in my fat thighs
I've known softer lips but
the passion there
betrays you
tells me how much you'll miss me
when I go
even if your words
will not.

I Know I'm Addicted

I collect boys
like pairs of shoes
fucking one while texting another.
I'm not slutty or desperate
I'm just a realist.
I know that none of them could hold my interest
if they didn't play off each other like that.
None could hold a conversation
about the prison industrial complex,
the evils of microwaves,
the importance of reading,
start up my weed wacker,
and make me want to call him Daddy
bent over wet, head bumping
the granite walls of my shower.
These guys
don't come in the same package.
The wise man Chris Rock once said
You're not going to find a guy
who listens to Wu-Tang
and watches Seinfeld!
I laughed cause I had one,
but his dick was too small
and he was inherently
unfaithful,
selfish
to the bone.

That Girl

You know the girl.
You've seen her, fat and sweaty,
struggling with a cheap stroller in one hand
and a dirty, crying baby in the other.
She mutters, *I'm a beat your ass, boy*
paying the bus fare,
squeezing the transfer,
God knows she needs that roundtrip.
Holding up grocery lines
with WIC vouchers and Food Stamps,
dragging laundry and begging rides.
Head turning as booming systems slide by
a promise on gleaming rims
I was that girl standing in line at AFDC,
and Housing Authority
angry and confrontational,
glaring at concerned white ladies,
judgmental black women.
Another white girl with a mixed baby
snapped
I hit a bitch with a can of corn right up
in Food Max.
Only showed my belly, soft and vulnerable
for the seductive lies of the men
like my baby daddy, here today,
gone tomorrow.
I was that girl,
but I'm not anymore.

If You Can't Stand The Heat

Even the trees look tired
the sad, brown grass about to combust

the Low Rider Oldies are singing smoothly
for the cool of dusk

It's tempting to start the drink now
but with the sun this high,

I'd be laid out with the dogs, panting
a gin and tonic sweating a glass with lime

reminds me of last night
how the boy was lapping me

how he grinds into me
my hips a bowl of oatmeal butter melting the middle
how he always finds a deeper spot

then my phone rings
and I need to go home, make up stories

explain the stoned look
in my eye.

In the Pit

It's hard to say
drunken confessional
A girl too young to be so sexual
too stupid to refuse, afraid to lose
the moments of attention he gave her
whichever he it might be
Punk rock or Skinhead bad boys, all older
lower than a prostitute
kneeling behind parked cars
and under sidewalks where the homeless live
So rebellious and folded into her fear
ready to fight for anything
except herself
selling out for malt liquor
and that fleeting moment
as the bottle passed
of feeling like part of something
knowing the physical as the onlyrelease
needing it,
even when violent,
to feel real.
Numbing one against the other
drinking raw nerves mellow.

Incandensce

They were finches I'm told,
the tiny, grey bodies in my pear tree.
The pears decorating this skinny tree
are tiny, too like toy versions of themselves.
Crab tree-broke fence- bird shit on my chair.
My piece of paradise in the ghetto
it is here I write poems about you.
Like the finches,
your body is small and moves
branch to branch
making keys, fitting locks.
Your chest cage
holds the torch you believe
beyond repair.
I believe, in sulphur and lime
capacity undiminished,
see the fire peaking around your iris.
But you are right,
it is damaged.
You keep a shade battened down,
tight on that lantern.
You are weather weary
and I am a storm that comes on soft,
voracious,
category five,
catastrophe.
I'll rip your shingles off!
Power you out!
Leave you uninhabitable.
Which you may already be,
swamp thing.
She broke you down,
left you all mushy under muscle.

And you push up weights push- heave- yell
and I,
I feel it's a front.
A wall to keep me out,
away from that bright tongue of fire.

Love and Other Blood Sports

I'm a loner baby.
I keep trying to tell you
my cock spurs don't come off.
There's only room for one
in the pit.

I lose feathers
head held high
bloody neck
my claws
razor.

Look at me strike
my red bronzed.
My black a mean sheen of green.

I mate and move on.
I dance around then pound.
My beak drills into soft bird skull.

A pecker I am,

to the death.

I Been Lonely

Pillows, black with mascara
weeping myself to sleep
after intoxicated drives home
foot heavy with disappointment.

But lonely's misery looks good
from the squeezebox of you.
My steps measured towards the door.
I explain myself, invite you,
apologize for going anywhere you are not.

I lie in bed wishing you'd go
room growing smaller
scraping my elbows.
Oxygen running thin,
you hold on tighter and tighter.
I need to put my mask on
lock-jawed, I'm searching for an exit.

I danced around the hugeness of your blue hole
Dressed it up in lovely garments.
Camouflaged the emptiness
inside your bronzed chest,
Fixed your every distress,
but at the sight of my back,
you kicked it all over.
A house of cards in a child's tantrum.

A long time ago, you forgot how to cry.
Left in cribs with other babies,
babies of her drug dealers.

You were still waiting
to be picked up when we met.
So I held you and fed you.
But you didn't grow
and I needed to cut the umbilical
walk away, breasts leaking.
This is not a romantic story.

I have known lonely and right now
alone feels like ice water in a wavering desert
a long ride with the windows down
a resting place,
for a restless tumble weed like me.

Making Love To The Minotaur

On our last night in the Bahamas,
we took the Ecstasy to bring us closer
maybe some sex on the beach
to erase the damage done
in our lives back home.

The shit came on slow and sick
in my gut like acid or mushrooms would.
It forced me to squat on the toilet
pushing droplets of pee to ease the pressure,
the twisting of poison passing.

It was without the usual euphoria,
my listing the reasons why I love you so
but not un-fun in this dark house
on the edge of the world,
waves crashing unseen
under a black pinhole sky.

I saw my man as a minotaur, a centaur
all mythological muscles
browned in the Caribbean sun
the wind howling over white rock
giant scorpions looming.
I was sure Medusa's slithering head
would spring from the Milky Way.

My Venus, nude wrapped in a sheet
we fucked on the porch
his face scrunching into demons
coconut masks
me trying to muffle my laughter

so as not to wake my parents.

His face above me
was all crazy white teeth
glowing hazel eyes
scared the shit out of me
I called him Terminator Cop
his head, melting metal
bullet holes reshaping the side of it
morphing in the dark
and I was open, wet, sticky, salty.

I tried to sponge off
with a soaked, dirty towel
sprayed perfume
gagged on the smell
ate butter pecan ice cream
left handed
to kill the taste,
but still I stank.

Somehow, he came again and again
and I did too
seeing patterns shifting
squares into triangles
into worms into ropes and snakes
all brightest day glow
like old school posters
I traveled the world's waters
swaying in boats
in hammocks
rode the wind
in China, Mexico
in shanty town fishing boats
bursting with color and fishy smell.

From the toilet, I said things like,

We really are in Narnia, Aslan
He made me roar with laughter,
trotting around making hoof sounds
creating a horse ass on his buff body
till I laughed out more pee.

With sunrise, we took hot showers,
had no sleep, but planes to catch,
customs to clear
and I wonder when we reach Oakland
will you still carry me on your back
pull arrows from your quiver
kill the beast
that lurks in the teal green sea
lay me naked on a star lit porch
love me
even with your face
falling off.

I Am The Lobster

I don't learn from mistakes
only bash my head into plexi-glass
like the monstrous grouper
staring at me in the Dim Sum restaurant
The rubber banded lobsters
climb the divider
squeeze through the small space
searching for an exit
they only fall
down onto the half-dead fish
we take pictures and smile
stupidly clack our chop sticks
Robert notes that the whole set up is like a casino
A pit boss raps his knuckles on our table
and a bunch of dealers wheel by
with carts of hot buns
we are packed in here
stuffing fat faces
dying fish

we've taken the bait.

Found A Pawn Slip
For The Diamond I Bought You

How much more fun
it was on the way up,
then this extended
fall.

Drove past you just now
on the street
recognizing
piece by piece
the clothes I'd given you
black Pea coat
black Jordan's
black hat
too late
with a flash of reddish brown cheek
my horn was slow
the pavement slick.
And me
pen moving blindly across a notebook
in my lap,

Now I'm texting while driving
feel I need to say
look
it's not all
your fault
I'm the loser
that picked you out.

who's cooking dinner,

and picking up the kids?
Did you find an apartment?

At a red light
I notice graffiti
it says "follow your"
with the symbol of heart
"Shiiiit, that's how I got lost!"

Moist Petals

panties drop
shea butter fingers
dip
I don't miss you at all
a lone wolf
I lean into new men
at parties
tall bodies
bathroom hallways

 a sharp knife I push
under tortoise shells
pry at tender spots
kiss strange lips

I'm pillowy in a size 14
a steak too big for the plate

I'm back!
Threw the plastic pill pack
in the trash
a cage
small enough to palm
locked me in a body without nerve endings

But oh baby!
I'm here/horny/hormonal
fat and wiggly as a grub worm
in a frying pan

You, Purple On My Skin

yellow fades
you fade
with the bruise you left on my leg

you send nasty messages
you lie
say my pussy wasn't good to you
as if it was my fault you fucked
like it was your first time out
tender little dick that couldn't hold on
couldn't wait for me
and wasn't satisfied with the alternatives

things are not one way
Friday night doesn't mean a bottle of Jameson
Your YouTube DJ set
pouring your heart out with Portishead
in the small hours

Things are other ways too
me throwing your shit out
me forgetting Jameson and Coke
Jeff Buckley
and the way you worshipped my toes.

Of Bushes and Wood

Here in the calm of Redwoods and Manzanita,
wood peckers replace jackhammers
but my technology follows me out of the city.
My obsession with body parts in cyber space
I'm sexting when a bird whistles
and it is remarkably like a cat call.

I look up expecting a man from a Brawny commercial.
The stuff of old pornos
Before we went straight to the penetration shot
I don't need the set up the back story
The moment of penetration is all I want.

The first moment I feel you
(stranger) brand new
never before having touched me inside.
I'm wet and rushing
but all I want is to freeze this moment
to press replay again and again
My fix, my injection
you plunge deeper, my eyes
widen, then glaze
till I feel like

an ocean
a fist
a kind word
a hurricane
a fluffy kitten
a slippery fish
pull my hair, make me squeak
and we'll tell the story
of bushes and hard wood.

Whale Fall

Have a good day at work, honey
sorry for my deadness

It's dark down here and oh so cold

Zombie Worms chew me blindly
Hag Fish and Sea Snails live off the white brick of my bone

I'm tired
let me settle under the ice
the withering glaciers

to survive the depths, one must carry a tiny fire inside
one must light their own way

In this pickle jar,
I am still
under swell, under salt

my vertebrae scattered

my building blocks
your stepping stones

I once swam fast, made rich milk for my son

Now I'm all clammed up
the beast at the bottom
I lay for centuries
Ice cubes in your deep freeze

in repose
while you flounder
while you flail, while you perish.

Wet

My life is bursting
I am a juicy fruit
I just read an article proving
that sex addiction doesn't exist
the proof didn't prove a thing
but they did say it's just a lack of will power
whether it's addiction or will power
I know I don't have much
I suffer from chronic obsession syndrome
(I just made that up)
I become obsessed
with having sex with certain people
if it's good I want more
and more and more
tonight I have a date with a woman
tomorrow I have a date with a man
the fact that my life
is free enough to make these two things possible
is amazing, beautiful, unbelievable
not so long ago I was tied down
rubbing my flesh off
against the ropes of a needy man
and his expectations of my saint hood
my mother savior complex
it bit into my voluptuous flesh
and only added to the flood of my horniness
when set free, I'm off to the races
It's not that I'm fucking every night,
it's that I can
if I want to.

Waking On Empty

first, pour in coffee, like gasoline
second, search messages
for validation

a robin out back gets a worm in the patchy grass (must be
the early bird)
I squint through eyes ringed black with mascara
at a shitload of adds in my inbox
Delete, Delete, Delete

what can I pour in next,
TV shows or books

stories of people more fucked up than me
that feels best, always

the lady who kept fucking her molester for twenty years
the guy who shot more heroin than humanly possible
and lived to write it
(someone must have stepped on it hard, Joe)

trying on other people's stories
makes me look good before putting my fat feet to
floorboards

checking the balance on my unemployment card
with no intention of a job hunt

and every intention of sneaking away
clean panties hidden in my purse

with a pint of Hennessey and a credit card

you are mad at me again, staring at the TV in the guest
room

as if the two of you were holding conversation

me and the tv can share you
have an open relationship

one in which I can keep my Kitchen Guy for fucking
and you for cuddling

It's horrible to say, I know.
You are low maintenance, you tell me, but that's not true

It's still babysitting I refuse to do
My lust, so strong at times

I roam super market aisles
grabbing things to fill my cart

planning meals like rendezvous
hoping the meat, bread and cheese will stick us together

the way it does my insides
even when its gone and the ice cream follows

or I tip toe in at dawn, his handprints
purple on my skin
I wake on empty,
planning my next meal.

Under The Covers

I can smell fresh-ground coffee brewing
dawns light, red through my eyelids
I squeeze them shut, imagine
hard nipples
69 racing through my mind
a woman's breast pump in her purse
how just the glimpse of it made me tingle
thinking of her closing the door to her office
removing breasts from bra
wet and heavy
how I would like to enter a woman like that
wet and heavy
how I'd slide in
make her squirm
in her tight sweater and black leather pumps

but I keep my back turned
offer only a cold thank you
to the coffee
perfectly sweetened
and creamed just right.

Un-Friend Me

You ever know someone
so stupid
they try to keep all their exes as friends?
I'm that someone
collecting and feeling sorry for them
as they crumble into pieces on my exit
but refuse to blow all the way
away
I have two clingy exes right now
it's unbelievable, the hope they
hold after being thrown out
both of them,
big black trash bags full of their shit
rolled down the front stairs
I mean, I washed that grey right out of my hair
but they still want to be friends
allude to things I said before
before, when I gave a fuck
they sit in homeless shelters
and sleazy hotels,
replaying our time together
carefully edited by them
to let them believe certain things
about themselves,
about me,
overlook the sex not even being good
the escalation of the fights at the end
the words that signal
no return
still the texts roll in
the misplaced memories
the land grab of love.

The Make Out Room

Tomorrow, I will wake up with a hangover
and the boy in my bed.
I'll look over at my muse
see his narrow naked chest.
I'll feel like Liberace
with my young ass men
I'll write poems about how insatiable he makes me
and how grateful I am to be here.

No longer in an angry room
shades drawn
a man at the end of the bed
yelling at me how horrible I am
the betrayer, the slut
I may be all of those things
but for now, I'll revel in
sheets on bare flesh
pulsing, springtime voluptuousness.

Dark days behind me
when I faced this boy at work
and he was off-limits to me
the worst kind of diet
when I promised not to touch him, to taste him
but begged him to meet me in our patient's bathrooms
call bells ringing, his mop leaned by the door.

I'm free now, tired of pacing
I sprung the cage, kicked down the door
I ate my interrogator, spit out his bones
now I pick up the boy or a girl or a man
just cause I can
just cause I can

The Lonely Hunter Beats On

My heart greets me
with a red fist
punches me
dead in the face
flutters around
like a butterfly
lands in the cabinet
plants worms
in my flour
sinks down
to my pussy
hungry, red, throbbing
lies to my stupid brain
wants starburst,
skyrockets,
afternoon delight
this is not love I know,
but my dumbass heart says it is
mostly,
what it wants is
attention
rubs ankles with a flirty tail
nuzzles your cheek
with a cold nose
longs
to be cracked open
like a
Christmas
pomegranate.

\

The Dress
was too small
it ripped up the slit in the back
a straight line up my ass crack.
Red and shiny
It was all that I coveted.

Could have been worn to a prom
if my boobs weren't falling out.
My aunt hid it with my boosted bottles of booze
when the cops brought me home.
I stole it from Macy's.

Wore it on New Years
it was nowhere near big enough
halfway through the drunken night
my ass was out.
Larger than life as usual.

I sometimes stuffed
too-small shoes
let the back of my feet hang over
Stan Smiths.
In three colors,
the only colors I wore:
black, white and red.

A drug dealer friend paid for the limo,
told us to a choose a restaurant.
We saved him money by stealing the drink
did lines in the bathroom
my boobs and ass peekabooing
on both ends.
The shiny, red material, useless,
uncomfortable,
ended up in the trash
and I wished I'd worn something my size.

Speaking To You Is Like A Fox News Interview

so one-sided
I'm a scholar, I say
I study these things
but you tell me I'm wrong,
that I destroyed you!
I'm diabolical
and you my doe eyed toy
make snide remarks
Write a poem about that, you say.
Funny, you turned in to my other ex
I didn't have you pegged as a mean drunk,
but I guess all drunks are mean
if they drink long enough.
You ask me what I know about it,
the pain you live
in your one room hotel
the dirty walls dripping Al Green
tweakers in the hall
you can't admit to being one
dope fiends always categorize themselves
as better than the next addict
that way, you can rationalize
kinda like how you're doing in the relationship
or lack thereof
if I'm an evil bitch,
you can sink into your dark place
rage over the glass pipe
while complaining about the dealer across the hall
your eyes, all pupil
the black of a hateful stranger.

Six Is The Nine

Your face
between my thighs
licking like a machine
I like to be locked
into contorted combinations
keep twisting me, turning
mold me always
squeeze my fat flesh till it's honey.

Six and nine
turn up in my addresses
my social, my phone
the circle of life
bend me, bend me
make me rubber
leave a stain
on the sheets
I will wash them
round and round
I will eat you
I will meet you
and we will sleep sated or sad.

A new day will start a new wash cycle
and on that day
you will be the nine and I will be the six
your head hangs low
my belly protrudes
we are better laying down
Pac mans or wheels of cheese
the other holding the missing slice
Whoka whoka
your skin is brown

mine, a flesh colored crayon.

All this living is exhausting
except when you fit the nine into mine
and we are off rolling down
grassy knolls into pig piles
for a moment, life is good
the sky loves us in blue
moons make promises that this
isn't it, that there is more.
That I will make love again
in a Venezuelan ocean
by moonlight
that next time,
the man won't be drunk
or married
or a soldier
that I won't
be worrying
about the polluted water
eating my flesh,
him giving me VD,
or mom watching from a porthole
anchored nearby.

Scars Are Sexy, Ask Anybody

I always liked guys with bullets under their skin
and shot-off legs
guys like Mac 10 and Marcus Law
these guys had war stories
and knew how to look a girl in the eye
like they would leave you with some
of your own.

Here is a partial list of my scars
the ones you can see
the ones you can't are far more incapacitating,
believe me.

When I was one,
a Newfoundland named Oaf almost killed me
my face disappeared between her jaws
my mother screamed to see her beautiful baby deformed
but somehow I was left
with only a hair-thin-line across my nose
and the dog remained my friend like her super cool hippie
chick owner
who wore cut off jeans
so short you could see her pubic hair
and always took time to play with us kids.

I pedaled my first bike, a blue and white Pony, downhill
fast as I could
hit a rut full of gravel and went down
grating my knee like hamburger
with sharp stones
limped home to show mom
a gaping hole in my jeans
and the ugly brown stain I still carry.

Got my first stitches cleaning a kerosene lamp chimney
spinning in soapy water, the glass bit into the meat of my
hand.
We lived like that, only a dim flame to light our way.

On my forearm, a small oval
from a German Shepard's tooth
a guard dog at our carnival trailer
brought me to my knees

At fifteen, I drank enough
to leave my large body
woke up in dried blood
piecing together my face-walking
way home
the night before.

At twenty-five, I left a boyfriend for his friend
he threw my cordless phone
split my forehead with a neat pop
blood hot down my chest
left a scarlet trail in the snow
in his other hand he'd held a knife.

And how could we know
two years later, another boyfriend
on another coast
would re-open my head with the same phone
to free himself
from my jealous teeth.

Ripping Up Marriage Material

An eyeball in a sand pit
Kneeling in rice
that's what love is like to me
My own weightiness wounding red
grain to bone
I beg to be lifted by armpits
Always in trouble, I try to talk my way out
A spinning firecracker, a hiss of smoke
Sometimes, we are good and drunk
A glass too many and I want to fight
You cry, face red,
too emotional, you say
Sobriety doesn't help much
I'm frozen
Can't glue my cracks
bleach my stained teeth
I worry you'll leave to get high
And I can't be that reason
The reason for you on the wagon
or under its wheels
Neither one
I'm an asshole, I know
But here goes; I don't like to fuck the people I love
It's too disappointing and real
I like to fuck people I don't love so I can pretend to
People married and locked up
after acting out
in a sweat, I pull my clothes on and I'm gone.

Queen Frostine

when he touched me,
twenty years dissolved

my cells have always been
made of cotton candy
but I had forgotten

I turned up at his door
shoe laces untied
blood rushing
voice shaking

dropped to my knees

all those innuendos at work
made toothsome

and I was
spun out in sugar air
night cold and sparkly

I stood
puff jacket shining under the streetlights
leaned up against the truck

kissed confectionary lips
neck sugar plum

trying to say good night

trying
to say
good night.

Problematic

All night, I think I'm super fly
I'm off a pill, heels sky-high like my head
imagine my waist small enough
to be circled by big brown mitts
I'm just too cute to be 43, hair waved just right,
bangs hand-cut in the bathroom,
bleach job brings back youth.

I feel so fucking beautiful in the car
singing old school jams
seat tilted back, freeway's concrete walls
wizzing by
the driver as high as I
the romance of San Francisco's lights
give way to ghetto, then mall land ratcheting by
freeway construction, faded white lines
and he's too close to the wall
but I can't die now and if I do,
at least I'll be feeling this good.

At Motel 6
Me and him, we've been here before
Samoans are fighting in the parking lot
and I clack on by in my ridiculous stilettos
hooker boots I bought off strippershoes.com
they had to come out of the closet sometime
in the motel mirror, my red eyes stare back
hair gone to frizz
cellulite and veins released from too tight pants
skin breaking out red
and glaring in the harsh light
no video vixen, no slim seductress.

Oh, Motel 6, get some softer lights
some bigger towels
my fat feet and the ecstasy are wearing down
but sleep don't come, we've soaked the bed
in baby oil and Hennessy
the smoke detector lays disconnected by the bed
weed hovers thick and sweet
and I have to work in the morning,
will tip toe wide-eyed past your door.

Organ Donor

And I said the stupid words
while on my back.
He stabbed into me
splayed like a corpse,
sliced open
I hand out organs.
Why would I offer love to someone
who cannot give it?
Someone who wants to "save" me
while purging himself of so much built up sin.
I gave too much.
The organ I may still need the most.
I'm not done with it yet
and sex was all I meant to give.

In Prison They Called Him Ojos de Leon.

He is beautiful, even in a dead drunk snore.
His skin, velutinous, never needs lotion.
He looks through golden eyes half-blind
intoxicating with their creeping greenness
and it's contrast on black lashes.

He claims to tire of compliments but mentions all of them.
He resents love, its conditions and its shortcomings.
It can't change his unlovable-ness.
So he numbs it with powder and booze.
He knows he will disappoint.
He knows that, in the beginning
we will see him as we want
rippling muscle and tattoo
voluptuous lips, waist, a tight v, ass, round.

At first meeting, he looks you dead in the eye.
Holds you.
His stare, a dare
to see him through his blunts and bottles
his three kids and counting.
He is still settling to his own murky bottom.
There is intercourse in his look.
He's sizing up the strength of your backbone
and like the lioness, you will have to work for this.

But all you can do is wonder
if he'll look at you like that
when you are underneath him
the moment his smooth chest
becomes ruddy
the tiniest goose bumps rising.

Motherless eyes say
you don't know
the river
of pretty-broken things
that runs beneath
the lion's exterior.

Frosting The Cold

Sometimes, you look at me
like I was made of cake.
You think I savor the story
of a good break up
and I tell you,
Some slices are better cut off.

I'm always the first
to replace the last!
You should know that,
before you go getting that look!
I'm not a French fry and you are out of salt!

Birds are crashing the windows again
drunk on dog food and grass seed
It's a cold new year
and my cynicism
has me all choked up
I put it on and take it off
with spiked necklaces
and skinny jeans
on and off
banana peels on the closet floor.

I don't know how to sustain desire
understand it only pertaining
to men who need to be seduced
lured with hooks in juicy cheek.
They only give hours of their time,
small pieces like appetizers
taste better than the main course.
And living together
I just don't know what to do with that.

My Ears Are Up

haunches taut
and I take words to mean things
bad stuff about me
even when they're not meant to
they whisper that I'm a cheater, a spendthrift,
I have fat thighs and lying eyes.

You thought you were being helpful
didn't know you'd hit a nerve
a hammer to my runaway thumb
but I was looking for a fight anyway
met you outside the shower
with fists balled and a bitter tongue,
I was just pretending
I'd lick you with it.

My Baby Daddy

The mythomaniac—
full of promises,
meaning every one of them
Cars, shoes, diapers.
Creature man,
his street name
sounds like he's rising
from the black lagoon.
I never got any
diapers, formula
or a ride home
from work the day
after I fucked him
and stood waiting in the rain.

Begird

I'm no bird
frankly, I find them distasteful
bones, too thin
meager and easy to crush
feathers too dusty
I prefer soap and water
for my plumage.

Me,
all flesh
round, a loaded shell,
smoothbore shotgun.

I'm big boned like river rock.

An earth animal
despite dreams of flight
my paws never leave the ground
they pound and they pound
so I don't drown.

I admire the sentiment
the folding and unfolding
your own little accordion
readying for lift off.

But I'm more of a mule in a quagmire
and damn, but
that carrot looks good!

I get rode hard, put away wet
keep a pistol in my muff
a secret in my lips

too voluptuous for bird beaks
to kiss.

Do you want to touch
the meat at the back of my throat?

more than words
come here.

Black Hole

The moth won't get out
flailing wings
astringent
in my mouth
I can't form words
my face is in his pubic hair
his hands on my head
the moth fights
fills my throat

which is broken
shut down for remodel

I want to whisper

Just love me
tell me
      I'm beautiful.

Can't Hardly Wait

in line shifting foot to foot
I mentally tear apart
the idiots in front of me.
Coming off the freeway
the same ripped bumper
hangs off the edge of the overpass
ominous
doesn't anyone pick shit up
in this town?
Crushed red and clear plastic
litters the intersections
we are all rushing
around
bashing into
each other
bumper cars trained us for this
season of lines
brake lights
and fools clutching packages.
A truck passes me
crushed cars
stacked on its bed
broken like me
and my mate
how we smoosh
our damaged pieces
against one another
hard sharp
we are stalling out
pressing the hazards
in the dark rush hour
crying for help.

Curled To The Floor

Big lanky dog limbs
too large for the cushion they spill over.
Makes me want to get down on the floor,
compromise with ass on pillow, head on floor
or vice versa.
The stove is close by
and something tasty will come your way
if you're patient
if you keep your eyes down,
a humble expression
around your wrinkled mouth.

Kicking from a dog's dream, I whimper

The boy I desire will be back.
They always come around,
Him, with his slippery, slim waist
hard, bony body
the better to rub my wetness on.

If I can wait
and not pressure him.
Bite my oven mitt
the situation is still hot!

If I can just stop,
my restless toenails
 jumping at every noise.

Bottles of vodka don't sedate this burning
I need sleeping pills
and some sense of accomplishment.

That elusive thing

that…

Something
to look forward to.
Without it,
I'm dead.

Fallen Fruit

We all fall to our knees
crazy, weighted, underwhelmed,
we all fall out of love
tired, bored and bitchy

We all fall apart
pieces of ourselves
scattered across the country
like tumbleweed.

We all fall
for bullshit lines
unpeeled, we are easily bruised fruit
wanting the sour sucked out of us
needing to hear of our own beauty
we spread our seed
we are programmed to do it
in need of pollination
in a world where advertisers
find new ways to sell us plastic parts
to enhance our flower attraction
and we fall for it.
We want straight white teeth
to run our pink tongues over
want bright clear skin
to entice a lover
we want and we want

And we fall
a little deeper
our dirty roots
searching earth
for sustenance
to feed the hunger in us
we can't even remember why
we have these empty spaces

what was taken from us
as young saplings
but we use and
we try to fill in the cracks
only widening
our vacancy.
Only rotting
on the ground.

Ferine

He eats me whole
foot first

No fear of dirt
or blood

I live in deodorant commercials with whistling bars of soap
and romps through wheat fields in crisp, white maxi pads

He doesn't mind grit
Washes his hands in mud puddles

confesses
he likes to leave my smell on for days

Inhale it when the shower's water hits him
makes him hard

He says,
Is that bad?

Wrinkling my nose,
I imagine my worst,
unwashed funk
and consider a feral love,
gamey and raw.

Fly Up

Bills pile
on one nightstands
outside the grass is dying
the dogs are rolling
the birds fly up. Inside
a 1-800 number
an automated voice
wants money
what none of us have
what isn't supposed to buy love
but does lubricate relations.

The cords are in knots,
hair of dog on bedclothes.
You love me, you say,
but you should hate me.
You ply me with cash when I am sad
I used it to catch you
when you were wild.

A naughty bird,
I rise from ashes
only to set more fires.
I wanted to build this nest
but I'm crowded by it,
ready for the hunt.
Your mouth is blinding
wide, hungry
ghetto child.

Your history is spoken,
mine written on page.
My whiteness unbearable
a culture of non-culture
clumsy like the polar bear
I'm accused of being.
Dear lion,
Dear king of the jungle,
please excuse yourself
with your messes and needs,
my wings are cramping and I need to fly up.

Kill and Save Kind of Love

Our fights were always over some stupid thing.
I ran through that building crazed
mazes of stairs and narrow halls
I'd climb out the window, up the fire escape
Dre would follow his slim six five frame
loping across the roof,
a strange stage for our drama and tragedy.
On the streets below,
people did normal things
like sell drugs and board the bus.

We punched, kicked, and bit
disagreements over cream of wheat
and where his time is spent.
Many times, he took back
everything he'd given me.
The most ridiculous:
a tape I recorded off one of his.
The most conspicuous:
a giant TV
bringing it back over the hill
every time we make up.
I was always throwing bottles
and burning things to prove love.
melted my ex's sweat suit on the stove
lit pages of journal confessions
in basement barrels.

I suffered his action flicks
took him to indie pics
Action Jackson hated it,
capped on it the whole time

and he'd laugh
my ace boon coon
stayed up every Saturday night
for Showtime at the Apollo
and we'd laugh...
the flo in joe
the fly in my sky.

My freaky-deaky baldhead
when he first saw me
in high school hallway
said he never would
but it was all good
platinum hair on a dare
22 bus, it was just us
kissing till slob wet our chins
he slid right in
big dick, bust a nut too quick.

He spit, I burned
a hole in his coat
never learned to stop acting over-hard
to show and prove love
don't you wish that bitch you married
was hot like me.

Saw them arguing at a red light
perfect little family supposed to be me
but I don't envy
she won cause I'm better at leaving.

Had my son first, light-skinned
slim goodie like you
could of been you
but it was a kick in the gut

the little picture of your son
you pulled over to show off
blast from the past
and still you want to throw pennies
at my glass.

Don't need your critique,
don't miss your physique,
you would have rapped smarter
if he'd stayed mine
even back then you were savvy enough
to detect my intellect reflected in your black dog eyes.

I found you in a dark room
throwing your stuff at the walls
your mother wouldn't tell you
who your father was
so I knew you'd never
leave me, but I still had the abortion.

My knife in your back
snuck brothas out fast
clutching unbuttoned pants, shoes in hand
knew you would have killed me
wanted your attention that badly
later you showed me baby clothes
for a baby that died
wasn't mine.

And I came to your mom's house
Bleeding, lied
on your mom's couch carved out by that guy
same one gave me gonorrhea
I brought back to Cali,
gave you,
we passed it back and forth,
but didn't admit to loving each other

got yelled at by the City Clinic worker.

Unprotected, I walked the line
for love to keep my head above
woke on a gurney
a fat pad between my legs
rows of us like a morgue
groggy I could feel clumps of blood
heard moans behind blue curtains
hiding hollowed holes
I need to get out
the life taker not the baby maker
I kill relationships and their offspring
run from coast to coast, never outrun enemy me.

Our life together would have been movies,
cream of wheat and Tad's steak dinners
what could I do but hate you?
move on, color you in between state lines
ignore the signs
you can cut me to my big bones
only, under disguise,
you still want to fuck me
put long E.T. fingers in my mouth
tell me to suck them.

Bring back something so ghostly,
it never was
and you tell me what's wrong with my life
you, record label owner, entourage loner
phony-baloney boner
held my tears in till you left
stiff to your touch.

Quit you for good after ten years
locked myself in the bathroom at work
where all of us sit behind computers

fragile eggs, too much time to think
fall into the ink
the slightest tap and it falls in your lap
soaks the lobby carpet
red eyed receptionist
not on the cleaning list
tried to put her back together again
what a loony bin I'm living in.

Labor Day

Had to be good
started in bed
late
a pile of new books
and a pile of dogs.

The big dog
being a guy,
always takes it too far
thinks love is enough
to finger feed his half chewed spit out pills
back into his meaty lips.

After I kick him out
my man comes in
a little stoned,
also known to be confused
about what I'll put up with for love-
he carryies a tray
to my bed.

Orange juice in a blue glass
oatmeal brown with sugar and cinnamon
raisins and Fuji apples
cut in perfect rectangles.

Two evenly-cooked, crispy
slices of bacon
spent lovers
across a square, white plate.

Lay Down With Dogs

Rosie digs a hole, eats dirt,
Chopper gets jealous, sticks his head
in the hole, licks the ground
she gets behind him, hops on her tip toes
wildly thrusting her hips into him
and I laugh, every time!
These idiots
are my best friends.

You were my other best friend
but we're back to being roommates
now slumping in silence
on opposite ends of this long house.
Before the mean, ugly mess I became
I thought I might just marry you.
Meet you with your friends at the bar
changed my status
framed us smiling on the fireplace.

But baby, maybe I'm just not your girl,
changing that "status" pealed my skin off.
I have tiny springs in my fallopian tubes
eggs don't live there anymore
and we couldn't even talk about that dry eyed.
I gave you, you
your own mother barely recognizing
your new, sober face

It's break up season again, so I'm out
with my plugged up tubes
and my carload of ex boyfriend baggage.
this hungry ghost can't be satiated.
I'm old already and no more the settled.

So I'll sit in the back yard with the dogs and the humping,
pieces of yellow balls in the dirt and the dog shit
and I'll laugh and I'll be old and I'll be alone again,
naturally.

Locked And Loaded

I gave it up at twelve
pushed through
no bloody hymen
somebody already fingered it out.

Old Grand Dad and Pepsi
lubed relations
I was always trying to get close to guys
that first fumble and kiss
the unzipping and inserting the bestpart.

I gave it away freely for about twenty years
and it's not that I didn't cum
or know sometimes they loved me
liked to see the white in my eyes
on penetration, the moan on wet skin

Still, I hid my stomach, saliva, spit and drool
the un-lady like gag
of throat and
pillow talk
Keep the lights on,
an old woman told me
men are visual
I took it to heart

when I met Black,
he held my feet
in the palm of his hand
kissed them beautiful
squeezed handfuls of my hip fat
and devoured me
like a pulled pork sandwich

greasing his generous lips

I was sprung,
not just on him, on the way
he made me want to be him
see myself through his eyes
live in my skin
for the first time,
my chin wet
looking up at him
calling me his good girl
I wanted to be that.

By the time I met Mr. Pink,
I had sensuous under my belt
but wanted him for his
good-job, well-read
politics and hipness
he wasn't a good kisser
but I knew
I could maybe work with it
eventually left him
cause
he left me
always
chasing
a boy not ready to love
the woman
I had become.

Mr. Brown came next
he was, I admit
a fantasy fuck
looking like a brother
who could do damage to a girl's

backbone
and he had the equipment
lord knows
but I fell for his brokenness
the mother-need
the abused child syndrome
and poured myself
into him
but the sex
oh God
the sex made me cry
left me fat and horrible
clumsy and fantasizing
desperate
and jacking off

I couldn't leave him
being that I was his
mother/woman
his everything/person
and when I
slipped and fell
onto
a body, young, hard
and gifted
got sucked into lips
and lifted back
into desirability.

With it, all the head fucks
and then worst of all,
got busted
too honest and too tortured
he held me over the fire,
well, they both did
the kid at work,

fucking his way through the female staff
at home, I was guilted
in a bed of bad
needled me, the whore
so predictable
and my sex was supposed to
go back underground
but it couldn't
it just couldn't
after a lifetime
in this skin

This
hungry, hungry
hourglass
time is running out
I can't lay still
stare down the cobwebs
over the bed
pull another fantasy
from my head
something to cum to
something I don't even want
but can use as a tool

like a tool
I feel
blunt and
ineffective
so, finally,

I shake free
at a high cost
naturally
rip apart a family
poison a man

confirm all his worst suspicions
of us
the meaner, weaker sex
especially loose white girls

These days,
I jet around
cum and go
and wonder,
what to do
with this sex

not like a tool,
more like a
weapon.

Losing Feathers

I fall back
naked and spread
white wings fold like hotel sheets
peach velour blanket on skin
bedside lamp shines on a Pizza menu
and corkscrew borrowed from the front desk
secrets wet the borrowed bed
voices in my ear
I turn neck into shoulder
but I know right from wrong
that it's silly to sleep with someone
I can never love
especially when each time
I trip and fall
on his hardness
impale myself blissfully
someone else is feeling the shaft
a blade in the back
tossing sleepless from nightmares of truth
I may comfort him
think him dumb
but he is sharp enough to sniff out my lies.
There is nothing virgin about my wings
they are tainted and tattered
as a gutter pigeon's
I peck and I peck
at the last bit of flesh
bewildered by the strength of my own desire.
It's a burn every time
I return

as much as I would like not
to hold the weight of his heart
it's gigantic throbbing pulp
I am flattened by it
can only snake out an arm
from beneath
text an SOS
plan another meeting of bodies,
even knowing
blood will shed.

Mount Diablo Is Burning And You Are On The Run

In this crazy place we live,
one stray spark, one small ember
it all goes up
the photos people are posting
so pretty,
a mountain neon red
a pink sunset mid-day
the brown fields wait in the forefront
for the red to meet them and eat them
throw their ashes up
up into the atmosphere
I guess it's always been here
this is just a reminder
to those of us who think we have it under wraps
our tender, little hearts packed away in cotton-lined boxes
we think never
never again will we let someone blaze
through our incombustible wrapping
catch us slipping into the ravishing
the crackling, festive music of it
we can't bare the thought
of us blackened, scorched and smoking
when the party is over.

Mussel Shell

meat again
my toughness
meets molar grind
incisor sheer
canine stretch tear
my soft body

the flubbing in my chest
the lies my head tells
I'm ugly, I'm ugly
the flubbing says dumb, dumb,
 dumb girl

I'm begging for
scalpel incision
excise this shit

and please
don't let me pick up the phone
don't let me speak
out loud
till it's gone.

The True (For Rusty Morrison)

A good poem skins you alive
leaves you flayed in a sandstorm
each finger of wind changes you on a cellular level
you will need to switch lipstick shades and wear high heels
with the excitement of it
they will enter you at a sunlit café
quench a hunger you rarely notice
one you've been feeding
with junk food and television
Slow your pulse
push you back through time
alone with grass folded beneath your naked cheek
like the first time you stayed up all night
your fiber glass eyes greeting first gloom
somewhere around noon, you'll hit a stride
realize you can push through
the aching joints and pink eye scratch
you are a machine aware
of all its exhausted working parts
your gastrointestinal tract greets you
and you hear what it has to say
the volume has been turned up on the world
observation kicked up a notch
you put on shades
but colors march like ants
leave you longing
but long past crying
these sense are more internal
or maybe
so external, they have left this dimension
opened a door to where your third eye has not been muted

with fluoride water and social media
the one in which the birds landing
on nearby tables
have something to teach you
and you are finally
ready to listen.

My Numbers

6 and 9
lucky
year of birth
horrorscope
reversed my son's birth year
or number 8
Daddy said lay it down
like a curvy woman
it spells infinity
we don't remember
phone numbers anymore
digits are saved in cells
lost with cells
come new with minutes
Rotaries as ancient as
operators plugging in
tangles of wires
party lines
princess phones
payphones, what are those?
brick phones, so retro
my number is Yin
and Yang,
black
and white
engaged
in sex
69
call me.

Pushing The Plastic

We have a fridge full of beer
left over from your birthday party
drunk can't fix the thing broken
you've gone back to smoking cigarettes
and just like my last ex,
it's in direct correlation
to me withholding sex.

The oral fixation, the pacing of the porch
you would allow my indiscretions
if you understood the calm it brings
it's mid-week and I'm still refreshing Saturday's sangria
adding alcohol and trying to push the last piece
of juice from purple fruit and my frozen mind.

My painter friend describes writer's block
as pushing the plastic around.
I stir a pile eight miles wide
a swirl of bottle caps and bee bees
dead gull's disintegrated bodies
leave only the pieces
colorful like toys in a gumball machine.

I'm stuck like that white trash bag
hovering over highway 101
the wind holding it in one place
a dangling jellyfish over speeding cars
over the blaze of traffic
caught still in movement
our break up and my words
suspended one more day.

Teeth

There you are,
and all those times
I wished for you to shut up!

I find myself searching
rummaging baskets of random stuff
loose change, receipts,
looking for the right words
to open you.

let me in to flat hazel

The unwelcoming flex of your chest muscles
shoulders angled the slightest bit
to deny me

and sometimes,
when I'm bitching,
I rant at you that
I need a break
from all the talk
wish that you would get out
leave me
now a
slow
saw blade
tears apart this room
each sharp tooth

a moment
of your silence.

Take Me To The River

Where slim boys swim
in their underwear wet dreams
silvery slivers of flesh in water
swing from ropes
slice resurface
turn into men
with memories of river banks
squashed beer cans
immune to the cold deep
the softness of cat tails
the fire carefully hidden inside
shy invincible
a head ducked
a sly grin
the firsts
kisses
slipping it inside
the heat
and mystery
the first piece
I wish I knew what that felt like to him
the going inside part
holding it there
owning it
my lover describes his first orgasm
the way his girlfriend's head hit the tub
still he lives in the body of a boy
never fails to turn me on
swinging like Tarzan
taking his chances with swift-moving rivers
just out of reach
He drops in
pops up with a wet grin.

The Spook Inside

PLEASE STAY AWAY
I say this is for your own good.

I am cold enough
to break you
over the recycle bin.

In bed, I will wrap myself in sheets of ice.
Build walls with my back
a door slamming, foot pounder, I live in the walls.

In the car you press my nerves
You are loud, sound ridiculous
can't see we are hurtling towards my past
and you are about to be a footnote
but you can't hear it over your own voice.

We've had fun playing house.
Now we play in the funhouse.
Our reflections, distorted red paint smiles,
can see the accident up ahead.

It was in the cards
I only have two good weeks a month in me,
the other two, something wicked
leaks out on my wet tongue.

In the movie we watched last night,
The Doctor's secretary said this-

A ghost is an emotion bent out of shape,
condemned to repeat itself time and time again.

And there was me,
naked on the screen,

broken-burnt,
haunting the closets of little children.

The War I've Been Waging

every cycle, I stockpile weapons
plan my escape

press flesh at the Best Western
a pill on the tongue

flying saucer eyes come in with the sun
and I never admit to my absence

Back me into a corner
I come with claws

leave me alone, they say, leave me
or I'll rejoice

in separating Adam's apple from throat
watching it roll candy apple red

I'll sleep in the wet spot,
I don't mind. Curl feline,

only my tail waving goodbye
I'll do myself, I say

you only get in the way
meat is good to my tooth

but without the hunt, there is no hunger
without the hunger, I will only waste away

 a paper maché version of me
you'll tote from room to room

show off big game you've bagged

When really, you've been spared slaughter

if only for another month.

Today It Rained Hard

Out of season
there were breaks
when the sun came out hot
uncomfortable in a thick jacket
I came home
got into bed around noon
as only the unemployed can do
we fucked and ate
ice cream with hot fudge
watched movies on TV
rubbing my aching breasts
your unwanted child
making me so damned horny
I think of fucking strangers
even now, when we're just done
Kirsten Dunst says in her movie role,
while crying her eyeliner off
and before getting killed by her husband,
that her father's advice was
to never regret the things you had done,
only the things you had not.
Said she'd had an abortion
and wasn't sure if that was a thing she had done
or a thing she had not.

Vano's Release Date Me Waiting At The Gate

When he hit the street,
Fields of Wheat
eat sweet
like Fine and Dandy
Cross Colors I sent him
for his Dress Outs.

Fleas and Ants pants,
Dickey Dirt shirt,
Oscar Hocks socks,
The Nike Ones and Twos new shoes
money in his Skyrocket,
I showed up in a '78 Seville,
the Rumble and Jar
straight from the auction
over the orange Golden Gate
into the sand-grey city
blue and crispy
home to Double Rock, rock
leaving Quentin in the rearview mirror
shots of Gin and Henny
pretty penny,
he fell into the funk
of the Elephant's Trunk drunk
wasn't supposed to be like this
Miss.

In my Shovel and Broom room,
we Goose and Duck quick

he doesn't pull out before God Forbid
he is laying it in to me,
promising,
 to make me his
Stress and Strife wife.

I, who
crossed that bridge on Sundays,
suffered search,
the squat and cough,
the up the hoop
oh, please pull back, pull back
watch your hammer and tack
wanted love
wanted his
Hampton Heath
beneath my naked wreath
please tongue my,
I Suppose
my red rose
my North and South
my Joe McGinn
his Lean and Lingers
his black Mince Pies
so full of lies
please don't split my
Rosy Bump

But he couldn't make love
was too busy possessing me
Me, I was his twist and twirl
his dumb ass Barclay Hunt Cunt
his ticket to Bees and Honey
his Brace and Bits,
I wanted to be his Mrs.,
his Cheese and Kisses.

no longer just a whisper
on the Moan and Groan
sprung from the Mop and Pail
and oh,
how he'd make me cry,
no longer calling collect
my expensive confessional
he ground me down
I broke the choke
busted the glass
and hauled ass
he proved his point
sprung from the joint
and oh,
how he'd make me cry
his twist and his twirl
and I,
I just wanted to be someone's…

someone's girl, someone's twist, someone's twirl.

No Wedding, Just A Funeral

It wasn't that my father died
parents do that,
when you are their child,
they leave you behind.

What brings tears on recollection
was the man,
the man I was engaged to.
He didn't come.
He didn't come, as I lay shivering
next to my open suitcase
a pile of blankets, thick
and useless on my shivering back.

He didn't come,
but told me over the phone
that night
in the frigid face of my fear,
he said, *It will be alright.*
Everything will be alright.

What perverse satisfaction I got,
less than 48 hours later,
as I typed out the words
black, matter of fact,

my father is dead
he is not alright.

When I Was Thirteen

My first love
lay beside me in a small bed
on a mountain top
A sea of wood floor stretched out around us
I told him it wasn't enough
his love, his worship
he was guilty, I was too young
he was scared, eighteen
and not knowing where he would go
he had decisions to make
and wanted me to make them
wanted me to say, *Marry me, keep me,*
let's make a house a home.

But I was already drinking whiskey,
fucking his friends
the wildness racing up through my veins through
the woods, the dirt roads, the darkness,
by lamplight, I cooked dinners on the
wood stove, spaghetti and pork chops, mostly
burning soy sauce and onions to cast iron.

It was already rising up in my windpipe
and I told him I needed to be free
I was graduating eighth grade
couldn't fit into this tiny class or be his girl
tired of shrinking, I was bigger and taller
trying to hide my sex on the yellow school bus
like I was going to drop some grown shit
on the green pleather seats
like it was hanging out my thrift store dresses
ducking behind my asymetrical bob
one shy, thick eyebrow to the world.

And I was trying to reconcile my worlds
trying to escape the captivity of them both
weekends in the city, we rode the T
to parties and movies like The Thing, and Taps
hiked up Mission Hill in packs
piled into his drummer's VW Bus

Mondays, I'd go on back to school
through orange-leaved maple woods
to a small schoolhouse.
walk a mile uphill
where I turned my back
where I felt it first,
the death of what I thought was love
the questioning if it ever was…

I like first kisses, the melting part
I chase the rabbit down the hole every time
but then I'm down there
down in it, the blackness
he's holding me, soaking my back in tears
salting my back, making me hard,
impermeable.
I turned off his faucet
I was allergic to his dick
he burned me inside.

He's the one to introduce me to that cold place
the place they all end up
He was my first and it comes back
to haunt the end of my sentences
like punctuation.
The question if it ever was
or if this is what it looks like
the end of love.

He's Right, I Do Hate
To Talk About Money

How much it will take
to get my car out the shop
how little the part time pay

I don't want him adding
mine up,
discovering
the minus
that lies
to the front
of my balance

I live on borrowed time
the way daddy taught me
never saved one red dime
spent everything that came our way

Welfare checks and trust funds
always some down time in between
but on payday,
it's always Christmas
so pull out the paper menu and get to ordering

I can't stand to be asked for it
but will buy anything you fancy
no matter how shiny and ridiculous

But please don't tell
this morning with no search for work
I bought champagne for breakfast
the raspberries, organic
indebted, still not very sweet.

How Poetry Ruined My Life

leave it to me
to write about the affair
to read it recorded
in public, blasted out
into the interwebs
where my man
watches me on YouTube
details of a fantasy lived
killed and revived
over and over
in a pink jacket under red light
my voice betrays him
he memorizes every line and lover's description
takes it to his heart-stabbing indictments
me boasting, he thinks to the world
how easily, how deliciously I slaughtered him there
with a glass of wine and a Valium
to keep my voice from trembling
was therapy so expensive
I used my audience
puked out my truth
expecting applause
leave it to me
to leave him
like this.

Falling
Into
Light
Head
(on sleeping with the poetry books of Terrance Hayes)

As much as I hate
poetry
the ambiguity
ambushing me
the pretentious
pirouetting
around
fact.

The book
I sleep with
tonight,
hoping for
assimilation,
words
held close
to skin

quickens
my pulse
like
Biggie Smalls
beats

washes me
in memories
warm like
washrags
after

sex

when he
cupped
my swollen parts

tender
glow of
brown skin

pectus
rise
and fall

my face
to
sternum

the breast
wing
combo

cradle
of torso
twitch

of
letting go

beefy hands
tangled
in my hair
go slack

and I

try to solve him
in sleep

wake up
between
pages

wrinkled,
like sheets.

Unruly

If the door is open
and my back to you

I might be able to love you
If you are ok with laying stiff under my grinding

knowing I hate the heat of your breath
prefer cracked windows, a cold draft

refuse to lessen the mountain of blankets
expect you to get the coffee

can you really love such a bastard?
see a future in my moodiness

a woman who will not tell you
anything

But spills words into microphones
fills rooms of strangers

with what should be whispered
in the dark.

With The Walls Knocked Down

I sit naked at my desk
knees primly pressed

see new birds
in fancy grey suits

outside
another dead cat

laid out by the dog
bloated in flies

I wonder what holds me
what any of the strings

mean
they don't pay bills

and I don't believe in love anymore
the actions of it

the two step, the tango
it doesn't add up

I don't want the end result
somewhere there is a mountain

beckoning me
one foot in front of the other

that is all.

There Are Words People Like In Poetry

white bone
smooth stone
pink tongue
orange yolk of sunset
There are words she doesn't want to hear
like, *What's stopping you?*

Stopping her are living, hungry humans.
She's lined them up like car decal stick figures.
Dad, Mom, four kids, two dogs, a cat.
Meow.
Words mom wants:
two rooms, a desk, a bed.
The small dog by her side.
Her own large, white bones
folded into the position of a fetus.
The rest of them
thrown out
smooth stone
rings water
pink flesh
of orange sunset–
her exit.

On Things I Did Or Did Not Do

After all those terminated,
before I was fixed,
only one makes me cry
even still.

This one rains down on me
twists my guts seppuku-style,
because of the pictures,
cell phone snap shots,
fat cheeked, hazel eyed,
exactly as ours would have been.

In my mind, she held the best attributes
of our other children
all water-colored down
all honey-colored movie star
or should I say,
Halle-colored
the tan all us white girls desired
the light skinned all you pretty boys acquired.

From the screen, this little cherub stared at me
innocent in her accusation
she was not mine,
mine was gone, mine never was,
vacuumed into an emesis basin
before its first breath.

Burgundy mucus promising me an end
to morning (all the time) sickness
and a beginning to the new reality
the reality that a decision had been made.

I begged you,
not to show me anymore,

and to not let me stop you
stop you
from being a father to her
whatever that meant to you
and her mother.
And you gave up on her
for all our years together
saying the baby-mama
wouldn't let her around me
and you wouldn't give yourself to anyone else
not even for a few hours
this didn't sit well,
not that I didn't appreciate your dedication.

It was the knowledge that you had turned me into
my mother, a costume none of us want to assume
my rage still bubbling at a woman too weak
to let me know I'd had a sister all along
too scared of letting another woman
slide a finger through
the rickety door of her relationship
wrap fingers inside where Daddy
just might invite her ass in.

But it was about the kids for me
its always been about the kids.
I did my best with my own son
and his half siblings
hell he has enough to start a baseball team.
And I was busy doing all this Suzie-homemaker shit
for you and yours.

I couldn't force you to go to her
or her to come to you
and then there was the other baby mama
I spent many a Friday night watching the kids wait

the hours slipping into bottles and blunts
or some young brother in an icy whip
whatever she was chasing
she let their calls go straight to voicemail
as if they were disappointing first dates
She was avoiding her own damn kids.

My plate was full, I'm telling you,
between us we could fill a bus
with our exes and almosts
our BMs and BDs and them
still having kids
thinking every piece of ass
held the promise of a real family,
a family built to last.
I was just trying to make mine last
and not be the cliché of holding you with a baby
like she tried three times dope.

In the end, when it all became too much for me,
you went and saw your daughter again
this time texting me the pictures
like all those other thumb typed daggers
about what a bitch I am
and why you love me so much.

Each picture cuts bloody
into a locked compartment of me,
one you're not supposed to revisit
after you stumble out of Planned Parenthood
each one hurts like the first,
in her car seat down on San Pablo
pretty in pink, ribbons and curls.

Her Filipino mom light enough
to have a baby that could have been mine

a gene somewhere that made it possible
for your crazy-colored eyes
to finally come through in your offspring
eyes like mine
that look so much
prettier on you.

This is the one
out of all that I've terminated
this is the one
that still
makes me cry.

Some Kind Of Way

I lived and cried
armed to the teeth
so much venom on the tip of my tongue
I had to stay drunk to sweeten the taste
disguise it in grapefruit juice.
Stood on tip toes dating basketball players
I pushed them hard
long bodies hit door frames
came out swinging
Bitch, are you crazy?!

And I was all kinds of bitches
and all kinds of crazy.
I'd be screaming in the
animal throat voice
beg them to kill me
I fought back mostly
and let's face it, I started it
resort to physical
when I feel
some kinda way.

Thought love involved boxing
the bob and weave
didn't float into butterfly
but sank stoned
red faced, snot stained.
fake nails snapping.
My fists' weak pound
helpless, dream-bound

he kicked me when I was down.

Like shit on his shoe
he spit on me, too
and I threw glass
so volatile, vile
liked the shatter sound
my whole house shards dirt-brown.

I'm all balled up in the closet
body bruised broken toes
after someone calls 911, the cops come
fingers bleed
adrenaline leaks out salty
belly aching
I pick up the pieces.

Space Creates Desire

Once, I wanted it
wanted to fill floorboards
with baby feet and dogs' clicking paws
couldn't do it
swept as much of you out as I could
greased your exit with Murphy's Oil Soap.

Now, I delight
in waking to an empty bed
barren sheets, smooth from the dryer
vacant counter tops wait
nobody's words circle with the smoke up the oven top fan
no door slams or hot breath on my neck
no fingerprints on the back door's glass
just me
quiet in the backyard
staring down on the house, like a visitor.

Think about it—
most of us don't really believe in marriage
but shack up
out of habit
and a need to share the rent.

Star Destroyer

Each day, the Yahoos come
whistling in
proclaim all I took away from you

each day, brain bolted
you list the things you miss

my head on your chest

    passing notes at poetry readings

drunk in the sand
    with Donna Summer

each day I ignore you
or Reply,
bumberfluff

you don't love me
you love the idea
of loving me

Sometimes, I remember
the dog walks under pink sky
all of us sprawled, paws over tail afterwards
with favorite TV shows
and twenty years' worth of movies
we wanted the other to watch

How did I?

erase you so easily…

Slide away like a neutron star

the answer is simple—

Sith happens

and out of your constellation
of understanding,

I want to be alone.

Skeletons Resurrected

I have written
the bones of them onto paper
spoken them
shamelessly in cafes and book stores
Oh, in the past my broken men
have thrown them
time and again
carved sharp to harpoon
belly up, I resurfaced
pulled the shaft from my gut
spilled the wine
turned the whole dreadful deal
into a poem
Let them clack their stupid jaws
and wish…
let them call me fat and easy
a cheater who spends bill money
on appetizers and drink
sneaks out in the sleeping night
for young smooth-skinned men
lately, I've been cleaning house
and the only thing in my closet
are new shoes
and I don't care
if I can't afford them.

The Scene, 1985

I came, looking for family
thought I'd find freaks like me
who liked music hard and angry
who couldn't write neatly between lines
who punched and kicked instead of dancing
hated everything
thought it was all dumb
music and art it had all been done
there was no new, no cool, no top 40 to aspire to
we were dirty
dressed in black
no ambition
but for the next drink
the music, louder
pain, fresher
it was realer when you got hit in the pit
then anything you'd felt before.
But they laughed at me
just like in school
just like everywhere
told me how to shave my head
what kind of boots to wear
I should have told them to fuck off
they were fucking up
my scissor-scarred head
but I wanted them to like me
and I conformed
not realizing the frat boy mentality had already replaced
Punk in Hardcore.
These assholes still wanted blonde cheerleaders
not big, bad ass girls holding up the scene
heads shaved, nails black
cigarettes and beers to our lip-sticked sneers.

Revolutions

They just completed the French,
then Haitian, moving on to the Industrial,
but isn't that a different kind of revolution?
I think, as I drive the plastic rental car.
And didn't they finish with Haiti kind of fast?
I wonder if that Craigslist boy
was named after Toussaint L'Overture.
I'd wanted to ask him if his parents
were revolutionaries,
if he was white and black or Latino,
But I knew he didn't want to talk about
a single thing from our real lives
only the fucking we did hurriedly
in his girlfriend's bed
the fantasy that I would come to his job
at the Hot Tub Shop
fuck him on his desk.
I liked the idea
but would never make it.
In fact, I thought,
wouldn't be back to his twenty something
messy, new appliance-filled apartment.
They were young enough to always
be out of toilet paper
but have piles of flat irons, makeup
and high heels in bathroom.
He wore his weed like cologne.
I was afraid if I went back, I would fall
 for their dogs, Cali and Boo
Cali was an older version of my beloved mini-pit
she whined at the door when we fucked
Boo was a retarded-looking, white haired Chihuahua

I also had a little soft spot for
I smiled over at my son.
Wished I'd studied anybody's revolution in
school, other than the Boston Tea Party shit
A revolution I could relate to,
wished us fat Americans had the hungry guts
of the Indians, the farmers
the people of Ecuador
who chased the notion
of privatized, Bechtel water
right out their door
blockaded every street
with wood and couches, burning tires, anything
shut the whole shit down
not this, 'maybe I'll stop by occupy after work
after I go to the dentist, after I get my rocks off'
kind of shit I do
not this, 'sign the petition on Facebook revolution'.
I hold all this in
smile at my son.
Glad someone is teaching him
something
as magnificent as the Haitian revolution
what he had taken away from it
was not to burn your sugar and pineapple fields
you might need them some day.
Nobody in my white high school ever mentioned Haiti.
Not in my black high school
either.

Popcorn

It's in his vocal cords,
his wide-lipped smile.
The feeling he gives you that you're on the outside
clamoring to get between those teeth,
that tongue that pushes happily against them
like waves in ocean
remind you of the first time you swam in salt water
how bright the Floridian sky,
the bikini of day-glow flowers
your flat little tummy sick with swallowing the warm swell
nose and shoulders, pink
sand powdering your body
with tiny, treasured shells.

His breath is like that,
like melted buttery stuff in rectangular red-striped boxes.
Hotdog buns toasted with just enough give to each bite.
How an ice cream sandwich tastes
after the dog hops into the bun
on the drive-in screen

John Travolta sings from the swing set,
Stranded at the drive-in, branded a fool
Sandy, oh Sandy, what will I do...

While Good Sandy sings to her ripplingreflection,

Hopelessly Devoted to You.

Cassandra Dallett lives in Oakland, CA. She is hopelessly devoted to writing stories, long and short. She is a Pushcart nominee and has been widely published, both online and in print magazines. She performs regularly around the San Francisco Bay Area. Her work has appeared in *The Beat Museum of San Francisco, Slip Stream, Sparkle and Blink, Out Of Our, Up The River, Hip Mama, The Chiron Review and The Criminal Class Review*, among many others. Her full-length book of poetry, *Wet Reckless,* was released by *Manic D Press* in May 2014.

www.ingramcontent.com/pod-product-compliance
Lightning Source LLC
Chambersburg PA
CBHW032040290426
44110CB00012B/891